To:
Victoria -
Love & Be

M000208992

INTIMATE
Thoughts

Copyright © 2011 by Darrin DeWitt Henson

Published by Darrin DeWitt Henson

Printed in the United States of America 2011— First Edition

Photography by Courtney Barron
"Disappointment" Image by Black Shadow
"A New Day" Image by Noobs
"Make-Up" Image by Sortdrame

All rights reserved. Except as permitted under the U.S. Copyright Act of 1976, this publication shall not be broadcast, rewritten, distributed, or transmitted, electronically or copied, in any form, or stored in a database or retrieval system, without prior written permission from the author.

Library of Congress Cataloging-in-Publications Data
Intimate Thoughts/Darrin DeWitt Henson

ISBN 978-1-937095-24-6 (pbk.)

1. Henson, Darrin DeWitt. 2. Poetry 3. Personal Growth

TABLE OF CONTENTS

FOREWORD   i

OH CHILDREN   1

CIRCUS   7

IT'S A NEW DAY   13

HOPES AND DREAMS   19

WHY?   25

YOU DON'T KNOW ME   31

WHY NOW?   35

DISAPPOINTMENT   41

Fight 47

Marriage 53

Mom 59

Make-Up 67

I Dance 73

Learn As Much As You Can 79

Future Kings and Queens 83

Throne 89

Aknowledge Self 95

Soul of A Man 101

Deep Dark Chocolate 107

What Will A Man Gain
    If He Loses His Soul? 115

Lift 121

Dreams 127

Award 129

As I Realize 135

Fear 141

Acknowledgments 143

This book is dedicated to my ancestors.

Jean Cochran, Hannah Cochran, Edna Henson, Frank Henson, (Grandpa) David Chadwick

My Momma Maude (Grandmother), Thank you for teaching me about the power of prayer.

and Mama Gracie - who helped raise me.

FOREWORD

During the time I have come to know Darrin (meaning: Great) Henson, I have discovered that he is definitely a brilliant individual whose work stimulates the soul. Darrin is a courageous warrior, who does not will to use any other weapon to excel in life other than his own authenticity.

One of the remarkable things about Darrin Henson is that, along with the imagination, pragmatic judgment and immense energy required to produce this unit of poems, Darrin is sensitive and profound. In just a few lines or stanzas, he transports our cognitive thoughts toward righteousness.

This book is long overdue. Its most immediate value resides in the fact that Darrin will provide readers with a manifestation of his feelings via thoughts via words and onto paper. As you read, you will gain access into Darrin's most "Intimate Thoughts" through his intuitive sense of the social and cultural complexities that often move the heart and brain simultaneously.

Dr. Maurice A. Lee
author of "Life Experiences"

INTRODUCTION

These pages are scribed to inform you of what really goes on in my head. From the person you think you know—the famous choreographer who created dance steps the whole world knows—to the actor breaking boundaries and removing myths about color lines. I wanted to share my process with the world.

It starts off with me at age 5. I knew I wanted to perform and the world would be my stage. Growing up with a mulatto mom and a famous horse-training dad, I had the best of both worlds. Seeing my dad in pictures with jockeys, from horses that won races and their big owners. It gave me an idea of what life was like beyond the Bronx. My mom, a little woman, with a huge spirit, was my first acting coach. That woman could put on a smile or create tears in a millisecond. A brother who was quiet and to himself who also turned out to be gay later on in life; or, maybe it was that way from the beginning.

An old woman named Grace Hops, who couldn't read or write. These people are the ones who shaped me, whether positive or negative, those were the playing cards I was dealt. In a society where it sometimes seems that there were others who had the complexion for the protection, I set out to prove that I was colorblind and I would teach others to view me that way. Inspired by the Jacksons, Michael especially, "West Side Story" (the film), "Wizard of Oz" (the film) John Travolta, Shields and Yarnell, Richard Pryor, Abbott and Costello, Laurel and Hardy, Gilligan's Island, Sanford and Son, Good Times, Danny Kaye and Lionel Richie, I danced and acted my way into your homes. Living the American Dream—whatever that is. I was determined to enjoy every minute of my life.

Throughout this book, you will encounter my poetry, the photography that captures some of my feelings, and an interview with me describing different events that caused me to write in the first place. The original poems were written by hand as you will see in the coming pages.

This is an account of thoughts that I had as a child to my adulthood. Just a peek into my world. I hope you enjoy .....Welcome to my "Intimate Thoughts."

-Darrin Henson

O Children

Sweet innocent young
For givin wonderous doubtless
Children kin to their
Soft skin smilin

Rollin on a Hwn from
Thoughts that persh the sky
Fly babies fly

Liv Dark bsian smart
we should follow for our
our future
we should sit and listen for
its your eyes that glisten
with possibilities of
Life without strife or stri
why do we forget that w
once Had that glow & s
yet But we mask and
and we lie and say very
alive children where art
Save us from ourselve
is torn from the Boo
read us

Q: "Oh Children" is the first poem in this anthology. Why?

—m—

A: In scripture we hear, "Children shall inherit the earth," and I truly believe that this scripture is true. As a child, we dream big. We dream without fear. I call this my first mind. My first mind is to dream like a child. If you ask a child what they want, they'll say, "I want a boat, a plane, I want a bike and a big house, and I want one of each for my friend, too. It's the first mind at work--without fear of inhibition. So this poem is really written from the perspective of thinking like a child because children will inherit the earth. That's what I truly believe and I wanted to start the book off from this foundational belief system.

OH CHILDREN

Sweet, Innocent, Loving, Forgiving, Wonderous, Doubtless children.

Soft skin, kin to their kin, smiling, Rollin on a high From thoughts that reach the sky, fly babies fly.

Light, Dark, Asian, Smart,
We should follow for your our tomorrow.

We should sit and listen for it's your eyes that glisten. With possibilities of life without striff or strife.

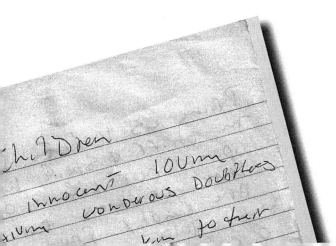

Why do we forget that we once had that glow and still yet, We mask and hide and we lie and say we're alive.

Children where art thou? Save us from ourselves, take us down from the book on our shelves.

Read us, bring us to life, remove the striff and strife we placed upon our lives.

Oh children hear our cries, our bellies are empty from the lies we've told in our lives.

Oh children save us, our hair turns gray from the stress, as be beat upon our chest, we brag and boast, but what we miss the most is the child in all of us.

We miss the child in us, the doubtless, the dreamer, the guided, the believer, the achiever, crawls before they walk, they cry before they talk, the process of growth stunted by most, only due to our ego.

O Children

Yes, I said ego.

Edging God out, which we can never do. Me or you or you or you.

Oh children save us, bring us back home, where the spirit of the young roam. No doubt no fear oh children stay there.

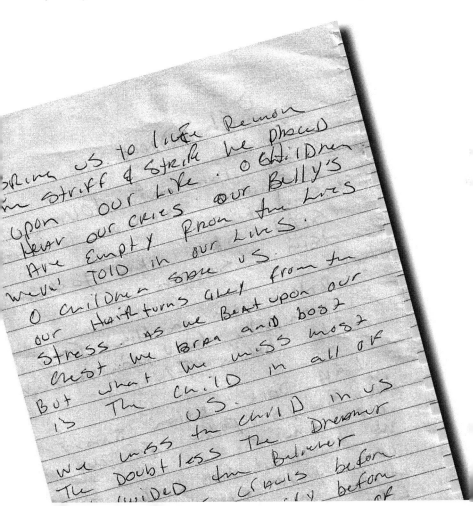

Circus

Where are the clowns
children come from all
around / to be entertained
where Lavander. Beasts out
Bein mundane. Show girls
elephants, lions, Show girls
& seals too.

~~strikethrough~~
Just about every animal
you may see in the zoo /
~~strikethrough~~
action Dancing clowns
out characters Just
you. / every childs Dream
see human walk on a
Rope beam / Applauds
2,000 Hands music
from is not filled
all fun all the time
wonders skills
flying thru the
y /

Q: Why is this particular poem entitled CIRCUS, and why is the poem significant to you as it relates to your upbringing and stardom?

—⁄⁄⁄—

A: For me, the circus was a pivotal experience. At 18 years old, after graduating high school, I joined Ringling Bros. Barnum & Bailey Circus. That was my major introduction into the entertainment industry. In that circus, I toured the entire United States entertaining up to 16,000 people at a time. It taught me showmanship, how to respect time, and how to be independent. It also taught me how to be a team player. I was exposed to people from Hungary, Romania, South Africa, Mexico and from all over the world. Working for the circus gave me the legs that I use as a choreographer. I chose to write 'Circus' in homage to my past, allowing my readers to know that dreams do travel.

Circus
are the clowns
come from all /
/ to Be entertain
Dance. Beasts
ions, show
too.
animal
the zoo.
clowns
cers Just
IDS Dream
on a

CIRCUS

Where are the clowns?

Children come from all around

To be entertained, where laughter beats out being mundane.

Elephants, lions, showgirls and seals too

Just about every animal you might just see in the zoo

Dancing clowns, acting out characters,

Just for you.

Every child's dream, to see a man walk on a tightrope

Or maybe,

run away in a circus too

Circus

Where are the clowns

children come from all

Around / to Be entertained

where Laughter Beats out

Being mundane.

elephants, lions, showgirls

& seals too.

every animal i zoo.

Applause from 32,000 hands
Music from a note-filled band
All fun, all the time
Two hours of wondrous skills
even men flying through the sky

For two years, this was the place that I called home
I met people from all over the globe.
South Africa, Hungary, Mexico, Bulgaria
And some even from Rome

I learned to speak their languages
That's what I wanted to do
I had friends who were clowns
and they were there for me

Never did I have a need to frown
In 1989, we were all Japan-bound
Tokyo, Osaka, we did live
Feeling freedom of life
Man, this was the best bid.

These things I hold true
Just some of my life I now share with you
Trust me, it may sound funny or crazy to you
But I tell you from my heart,
It's all true.

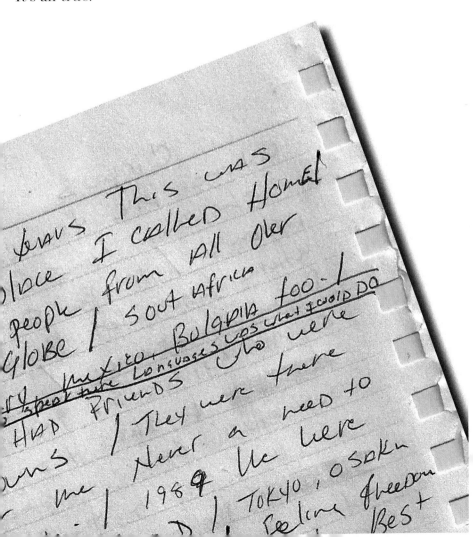

new DAY

...ith the breath of Life.
...to the Almighty Almighty Thru
...k with my pen. The ball AS
...balls of my feet I will write
...it heet the ink flows like the
...u my brain I will say it again
...es Due to the Almighty Its
...y Hightered place with unlimited SpAce
...s from the freedom come on LetS
...gets Some of this new DAY
...n way to Say thank you
...trent is your Highest praise These DAYS
...lluyah to the most high all of our
...ses like strong scent senses trent protect our
...homes flesh & blood Here our Spirits
...tome. Its a new DAY move forward but
...Dont forget the past ANcestrial movements
...orever host energy never Dies Dont
...Believe the monsterous controled EnviremntA
...   LIVES Its Anotur new
DAY   Do what you will itsUP 2 you to tal
the HEDOr love pill but for the Natur...
is the way to go Herbs, Detoez Activate
charcel. Clean out your temple Surge
          DUST of the PAST eyes open Her...
          Its A new DAY! strong
                              your

Q: What is the sentiment behind IT'S A NEW DAY?

—᷎—

A: I was taught that if you drive your car forward while looking behind you, you will definitely crash it. Very simply, this poem is about taking the opportunities we have to be better today than we were on yesterday. Today we can live without regret. A new day is an opportunity to grow. A new day is an opportunity to embrace the now. Looking in the past will only exacerbate one's desire to move forward.

Its a new DAY
...oke up with the Breath of Life.
...utations to the Almighty Almighty Then
...will speak with my pen. The BALL AS
...in the balls of my feet I will write
...d keep it heet The ink flows like the
...ood thru my BRAIN I will SAY it again
... prases Due to the Almighty ITS
...lonely Hightered place with unlimited space

IT'S A NEW DAY

I wake up with the breath of life
Salutations to the Almighty.
Alrighty then,
I will speak with my pen.
The ball, as in the balls of my feet
I will write
And keep it neat.
The ink flows like the blood
through my brain
I will say it again
And again
And again.
All praises due to the Almighty
It's a lovely heightened place
With unlimited space
Growing from the freedom

Come on, let's all get some
...Of this new day

What a way to say, "Thank you."
If that is your highest praise
These days,
Hallelujah to the Most High
All of our senses,
Like strong, picket fences
That protect our homes,
Our flesh and blood,
Where our spirits roam

It's a new day.
Move forward, but don't forget the past.
Ancestral movements forever last
Energy never dies

Don't believe the monstrous controlled
environmental lies.
It's another new day
Do what you will,
Its up to you.
To take the red or the blue pill

But for me,

natural is the way to go.

Herbs, detoxes and activated charcoal

Clean out your temple

Sweep off the dust from the past

Eyes open,

Head up,

Walk Strong

It's the first day of your fast.

It's a new day.

Its a new DAY
up with the Breath of Life.
...ons to the Almighty Already Then
I speak with my pen. The ball As
the balls of my feet It will write
keep it heet The ink flows Like the
...thru my Brain I will say it again
...ases Due to the Almighty Its
...ly Highened place with Unlimited Space
...s from the freedom come on Lets
gets some of this new DAY
...n way to say Thank you
...nt is your Highest praise These DAYS
...h to the most high all of our

Hopes & Dreams

Hope to Have my Dreams
come true
no Truth comes when
Dreams are realized
what is the Truth
what ever you think it is
my Dream is to realize it

Hope. Hope.
Hope Hope Hope
But Hope is to realizement

Dreams that travel at the
speed of light always inside
always upright always
illuminous and Bright + follo
for that will take you to
Travel amongst The Stars
or below the earth or show
Travel fast or s
our Dreams are rememb
of our Birthright t
cause our insa
Reasons. Listen
average feel it e
with the

Q: If you were speaking the lines of "HOPES AND DREAMS" to young children, what would you hope that they take away from the manifestation of your hopes and dreams?

—⁂—

A: Speaking to children is reciprocal. When we teach them, they teach us. I would hope that they would be encouraged to continue on in the pursuit of their dreams, to never allow anyone to taint them. Our reality is created by the energy that we put behind our ideas. I would encourage children and all people for that matter, to maintain your dream by putting energy behind it. Don't procrastinate. I would tell them, "May you live as much as you want, but never want as long as you live."

& Dreams

Have and Dreams

thin

us un

realized

Inotu

nk it is

realizing

Hope.

a trem x

at tim

ts insign

s

follow

u there

s

s

r

HOPES & DREAMS

I hope to have my dreams come true.

Truth comes when dreams are realized.

What is the truth? Whatever you think it is.

My dream is to realize my hope.

Hope

      Hope

           Hope

My hope is to realize my dream.

Dreams that travel at the speed of light.

Always in sight.

Always upright.

Always luminous and bright.

Follow for they will take you there.

Travel amongst the stars or below the earth.

Travel fast or slow

Our dreams are reminders of our birthright to our cause.

      Our mission.

Our reasons to listen to the energy.

Feel it.

Embrace it.

Move with the power of knowing. Be fearless.

Be courageous.

Just be.

Be a cause that affects great nations to be better at realizing their dreams.

Hope for a better day that creates a better tomorrow. My dream is my right hand that bangs the gravel of truth.

My truth. What's yours? I hope you find out.

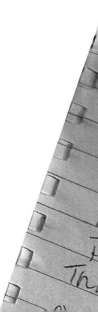

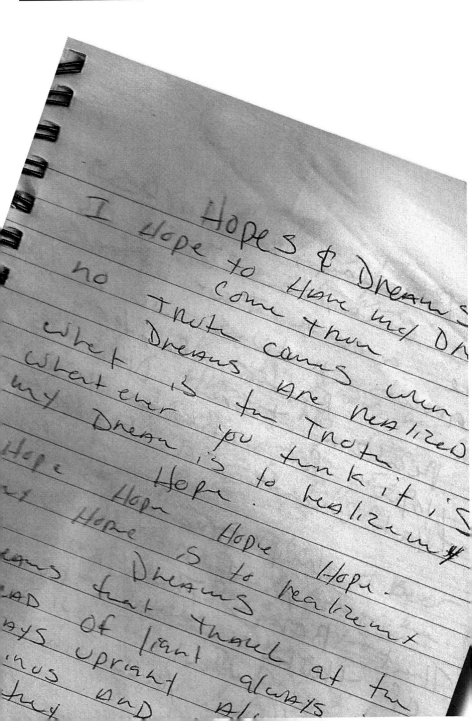

we Regret

ose. Bach
I'm Reflect -
we show neglect -
we work Like a
ith a yoke Aroumbitnuk

to we show lack of respect
come again!
rother man Bless up respect

need to write Because
want on my mind is burnin
hole in my skull
it's not For null it's for u
it's for us sign me! The
need to stop the cerebri
mental Bleed. But
want to scream an
and cause the fue
around again to writ

Q: You have one poem entitled WHY and every line begins with that word. What was on your mind the day you wrote this poem?

—ɯ—

A: The day that I wrote this poem I was searching for answers. I began by asking myself the question, "Why?" I found that when you answer it, the questions are unending. If you ask a question and its answers are infinite, then the real answer is "BECAUSE." Just because. When you break down the word because it's be-cause; be a cause. We must learn to BE a CAUSE to every WHY question that someone asks us. BE a CAUSE.

WHY DO WE REGRET
NOW I'm BACH
DO WE RePL...
DO WE
WITH

WE S...
C'on...
WHEN

cer'...
MY
a
HOLL
S...
teP
eD.
Screem...
...ture are
...h the aw...
...t to th...
...the ground!
...y Say I would
...Peace.

WHY?

Why? Because I said so.

Why? Because I talk too fast or you listen too slow.

Why are these people bothering me?

Why do you want the time I need for me?

Why do you ask me to do what you can do for yourself?

Why do you put your idea on the shelf?

Why ask why?

Why do clouds float amongst the sky?

Why do planes fly in the sky?

Why ask why?

Why do we forget?

Why do we regret? Pause.

Okay, now I'm back.

Why do we reflect?

Why do we show neglect?

Why do we work like a cow with a yoke around its neck?

Why do we show lack of respect?
Come again, brother man, bless up…respect.

I need to write because what's on my mind is burning a hole
in my skull.
It's not for null, it's for you. It's for us. It's for we.

The need to stop the cerebral mental bleed.
I want to scream but I can't, cause there are people around
in the air.
I have to wait til the plane lands on the ground.
Why? Because they say I would be disturbing the peace.
  Peace.
     Peace.
       Peace!

That's what I'm trying to do
Release, so I can find peace.

They say it's all around, but I don't hear the sound, Why?
Cause maybe the sound is so low, or maybe I listen too slow.

Regret

| 26 |

Whatever the reason, I know there is a changing of the seasons. Why? Because God made it that way.

Why you ask? I say why ask why.

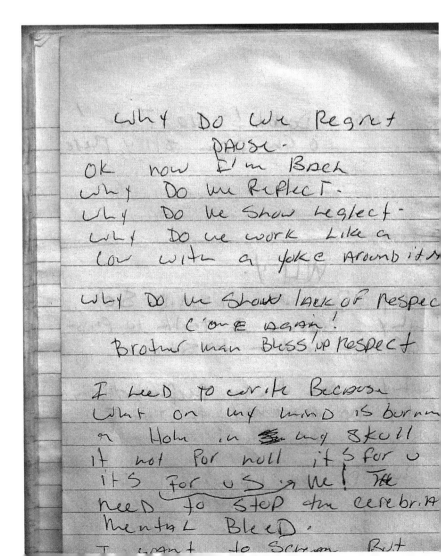

~~████~~ U Think

__Know me.__

You think You know me!
You Have No Idea.
Your Drunk with Ego
your mind is filled
with Poisoness
time Run Vodka d Beer
you think youknow me.
ont be PresomAtion
xt you Dare
What I Didn't Coe
you Live with
AnD I with me
of I . iTs US iTs We
ree of bet ~~████~~
Be is mE. Be

Q: Give me the background story for YOU THINK YOU KNOW ME. I understand that it was birthed out of your frustration, correct?

—〰—

A: I wrote this simply as a response to people who would judge me without having met me or spent any amount of time with me. I felt I was being unfairly treated by the things that were being said about me on the Internet. I had been warned by Jennifer Lopez not to read tabloids or pay any attention to gossip but you can't help but to read them. You want to hear what people are saying about you. What I read wasn't nice. When I read them, I became upset. That was my response. I couldn't scream at the world but I could write. I could use the pen and paper as my sword, and this poem was my way of fighting back. In our society, we don't know the power of our words. Few people retract them. Even the great Muhammad Ali apologized for how he used to taunt Joe Frazier, and I felt in this way, it was important for people to know, "if you want to know me, talk to me." But don't judge me if you've never stood in my shoes. Judge not lest thou be judged.

YOU THINK YOU KNOW ME

You think you know me

You have no idea

You're drunk with ego

Your mind is filled with poisenous wine.

Rum, vodka and beer

You think you know me.

Don't be so presumptuous, don't you dare.

Take what I didn't give you

You live with you and I with me.

I and I. It's just us.

It's we

Live free and let them just be.

Just let me be me.

Be all I can be.

And all I can be is me.

ow

you couldn't see me its I was before
attonolly knocking on my door Dawn its you
Lime once again drying to raise your
it its not a game you most be
cause I All you aint taken nothin in over
wake d little confusion with the fear
low figure love for self so I put
PRODUCTS Back on the Shelf

new and Improved Bread
are plentes non belivers crooks
frake-Hommes I told you before
cont know the New spend
the second on what you think
OWN ME I care of my
from the bondage thatis
self pity E dont belong
I am fro choice
or my voice
Listen to the Rytim
a you. A Natural
ways are
Its

Q: What were you going through when you wrote WHY NOW?

—∞—

A: WHY NOW is about a really bad breakup with some-one who finally woke up. But by the time she woke up, it was years later and she was full of self-pity. She wished that she was able to reverse her decisions so that we could go back to being in a relationship again. But my response was simply: "Why now?" It was too late. I had gotten over her. I have moved beyond the relationship. This was my way of allowing myself to accept what is, and to be okay with it. The poem was my way to acknowledge my own growth and the process that we all have to go through. Yes, it may be painful; but any form of growth is associ-ated with some kind of pain.

...was Before

...again it's you're

...gonna try... to raise your

you aint taken nothin over

...the confusion with the fear

love for self so I put

...back on the Shelf

Improved Brand

...non believers crooks

...I told you...

...new...

...me to...

...pathe...

...to hear

WHY NOW?

How come you couldn't see me as I was before?

I hear opportunity knocking on my door.

Damn.

It's you on the sideline once again

Trying to raise your score.

But it's not a game

You must be mistaken,

Cause you ain't taken nothing over here

I removed all the confusion; all the fear.

I now have love for self

So I put your products back on the shelf

I deal with a new and improved brand

No more phonies

Non-believing crooks

Or fake-homies

I told you before

You don't know me

Never spend another second on what you think you owe me

I care only for myself

Free me from the bondage that is called YOU.

Free me from self-pity

I don't belong to that political party

I am pro-choice

Now listen to the sound of my voice

As I say bye, so-long,

Listen to the rhythm of a new song

A tone, a natural vibration

Your synthetic ways are pathetic to my natural ways

It's time to hear the hospital's last chime

As tears fall from your eyes

What Now

How come you couldn't are the #5 T

I Hear opportunity knocking on my door
on the sideline once again drifting to
score a BUT its not a Gimme you mo
mistaken BUT its cause
Here I remaked All you #int taken
I now figure little confusion is
Your PRODUCTS BACK On the she
ol with A new AND Improved Bre
No more Plenies non believers
of Fake Houmies I told you
You iont know me NEW S
another second on what you
I Free me you OWN ME I care of my
Free me Of Self Pity
Political party I
to th

DISSAPOINTMENT

SUBSiquenTLY it comes So many way
it often Rears its ugly Head
once twice thrice it comes
an knocks Down over and under
Is IF I was Being Beaten in
HeaD.

DiSAPpointmenT FeeLs like a miGRain
is Heavy As a BUilDing
DOWN its POWnDing On my Brain
it screams loud &
on the weakest parts
It Snatters our Dreams
the Life out of our
PAUse. StOp-
on The Brink OF construing
No! I Dont know
I Take away
life OOZing

Q: Of course, all humans experience DISAPPOINT-MENT. What's the backdrop to that story?

—᷅᷄—

A: In life, people and circumstances will disappoint you. When I was in the 4th grade, I had a little buddy, a little kid who might've been in the 1st grade. I'll never forget— he was light skinned with freckles and red hair, his name was Jermaine. We went on summer break and came back and the teachers told me he was hit by an ice cream truck over the summer. He was dead. That was very disappoint-ing to me. These are disappointments that happened in my life, but this poem was a way for me to remind my-self and others that there is light at the end of the tunnel, as long as you keep walking. The sun always shows up. Even when it goes away, the moon comes out and we can see it because it is reflected through the sun. There's al-ways a little light there. You've just got to be able to look and see it.

So many ways

...in... Days

...s val...

thrice

...own

...s BE

eels

...uy

...POW

...s opt...

it sc...

the peace...

...on the weak...

It snatches our Drea...

...the Life out of our

...eezes — pause. STOP-

I am on The Brink

...ss No! Of constrlctq

estruction No! Of construtty

attitude I Dont know

Di- To Take away

...the oozing

to penaflate

DISAPPOINTMENT

Disappointment comes in so many ways,
Subsequently in so many days.
It often rears its ugly head, once, twice, thrice

It comes and knocks down over and under
As if I was being beaten in the head.

Disappointment feels like a migraine that is heavy
As a building pushing down on my brain

It voices its opinion when unwarranted
It screams loud and disturbs the peace.

It releases its venom on the weakest parts of us.
It snatches our dreams and squeezes the life out of our happiness.
Pause
    Stop
       Think

I am on the brink of destruction.
No, I am on the brink of construction.
A new attitude, I don't know this old dude.
Di-to take away, sap-this is the oozing ointment that is trying
to penetrate my positive outlook.

Regardless of what outcome presents itself
Pause for the cause, because I will ignore the negative diss.

My life isn't or aint about this.
It's about all of that other stuff.
I'm back serious as a heart attack.

I stand up tall, strong and straight
The D man is back
Now that's a fact.

Just sit back and relax.
Vibe to these words
like you were listening to Maxwell
or D'Angelo rocking on a track

DISSappointmen

Dissappointment coms in so

Subsiquenty in so

It often Rears its ug

Once twice thrice over

on knocks Down over

as IF I was Being Be

The Head.

Dissappointment feels like a

That is Heavy as a buildin

pushing Down POWNDing on my

It voices its opion when

uncoorrurted it screams loud &

Disturbs the peace it Reaheses

it venom on the weakest parts

of us. It Snaters the Life out of our

And squeezes the Life out of our

Happiness — Pause. stop-

think— I am on The Brin

of Destruction NO I OR

A New attitude Di— I

this DuDe

SAD

FiGHT:

I want to fight til cu

I want to fight comes

I Hate so much anger in me

I want to Broke things

I want to change the shap

with crystal glasses into Shatter

peaces of sand

maybe it's because

want to lay on a Beach

want to fight til change

comes

Because I am angry at

the caucasians did to us

Brown Ancestors

the theory Done to me by

Lying cheating Stealing

investors.

want to fight til change

comes

war B

Q: FIGHT has many meanings to you, but what does this poem mean for the African-American male? What does it mean for the injustices that you have experienced in the world?

—ɯ—

A: *Fight is synonymous with the African-American male struggle in this country. Fighting doesn't necessarily mean physical but more of a spiritual, mental and intentional fight that we go through. Whether it is adversity, injustice, a fight for power or against sociological ills, we have to FIGHT. We can't give up. We have to persevere. We have to keep moving forward. We have to understand that our will, our intention, and the energy we use to put forth to making the world better, for me, for you, and the greater good — comes from a strong fight. When we fight, we have to train. We have to eat right. We have to think right. In other words, we have to condition ourselves for the fight.*

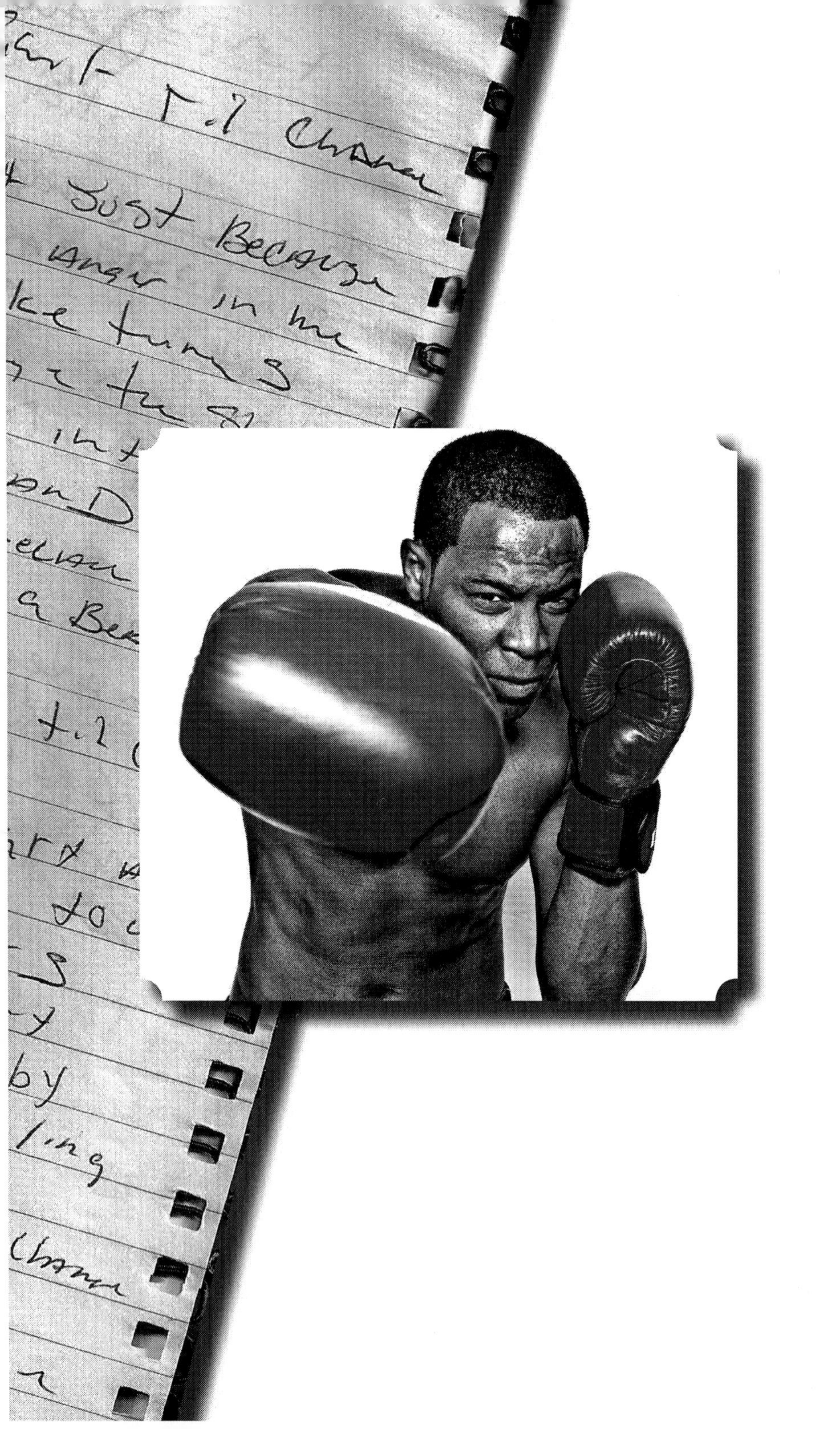
Just Because
anger in me
by

FIGHT

I want to fight til change comes

I want to fight just because

I have so much anger in me

I want to break things

I want to change the shape of the crystal glasses

Into shattered little pieces of sand.

Maybe it's because I want to lay on a beach.

I want to fight til change comes.

Maybe because I'm angry at what the caucasians did to my

brown ancestors.

Or maybe the thievery that was done to me by those Lying

     Cheating

        Stealing

           Snake-like investors.

I want to fight til change comes.

Maybe because war brings change.

Or maybe because I don't have enough change

For the meters that eat the quarters every seven minutes.

Click

    Click

        Click

The violation meter goes
That violates my right to earn a living
And instead of giving me more time
You want to take my dime.
No, excuse me, my quarter.
I no longer have enough to buy my water that I need to quench my thirst for justice.
It's just us til the meter maid comes to write a ticket. Should I pick it?
Is it worth the fight.
Is it wrong or right.
To take food out of my babies mouth,

No not tonight,
Fuck it, I'll just fight.

I don't have to worry about my arms being too short to box with God.
The Almighty is always on my side.

Fight

You should worry about the fight.

I'm spiritually guided.

Im in the right.

God

      The constitution

            My will

Fuck it, I'll stay in the fight.

My brown ancestors fought and I will fight.

The thieves come in the middle of the night.

I sleep with one eye open.

Scoping and looking for a chance.

But yet and still coping with the thought of the bell ringing.

Round one

      Two

            Three and four.

Injustice is knocked out.

As I stand and endure the fight.

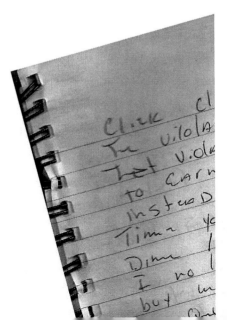

TO honor and Respect TO Love & witho
on whats right make sure to make whers
Our moments time spent We choose to
ke. Our walls cry out from tears of
from the essence of our energy
arch Deep into your soul Time
Like our DAY One Day like
As I think of thoughts about you
A horse at the closing Stretch
A touch to look often I wanna
on your kneck Its Thicky when
red Hickeys to Show our Affecteo
no Dear If you wish
Sow my signs of our decision of
from up Above. Living
nity Blessed forevermore.
Knocks on our will
An affectude of Gratitude I mean
scribed gift it Ascends and Lifts

Q: MARRIAGE is an interesting phenomenon. As a single man, what have you learned about marriage, and what inspired this poem?

—∞—

A: When I wrote this, it was during a filming. Two friends inspired me to write that poem: the director/writer, and her husband—who was the producer, Mr. and Mrs. Bailey. Watching them work together and support each other on that film just really bought a smile to my heart. That's what really inspired me. My desire for my own future wife is in that poem as well. Marriage to me is not about a certificate. It's about an understanding and an OVERstanding; an agreement that two individuals share, believe in, know and acknowledge between each other—it is what they stand for, live for, and die for. It's their joining. That's what a real marriage is to me—an agreement to be one.

...pect TO Love & witahold
make sure to make whens
t the spent we choose to
cry out from tears of
...scen of our energ
...s to the walls
...your soul
... one Da...
of thoug...
the clos...
often I

Its Thuu...
show our
if you c...
of our D...
Above. Li...
forenern...
on ourcu...
of creat...
to mea...
as Lif...

MARRIAGE

Our agreement to honor and respect

To love and withhold neglect

Reflect

On what's right

Make sure to make what's wrong, undetectable.

Our moments

Time spent we choose to make unforgettable.

Our walls cry out from tears of joy when we make Love

The essence of our energy can be felt from the windows to
the walls.

As I look and search deep into your soul

Time disappears

1 min is like one day,

And one day like a thousand years.

As I think of thoughts about you

My mind races like a horse at the closing stretch.

Anticipating a kiss

    A touch

        A look

Often I wanna kiss two soft spots on your neck.

It's tricky

When we were kids

We placed hickeys

To show our affection

Now we say yes love or no dear or if you wish.

Their all growing

Seed sowing

Signs of our detection of proven Love.

Gifts given from up above.

Living in the future

Knowing now is blessed forever more.

We always say

When opportunity knocks on our wide door

We open it with an attitude of gratitude.

This our friends is a scribed gift

Meant to guide your spirit

As it ascends and lifts

     Lifts

         Lifts!

Peace and be well

... flect ... Tree
strong undect ...
make on forget ...
Joy when we ...
can be felt ...
As I look and ...
Dssapears when ...
A Thousand years ...
my mind Races Like ...
anticipating, a kiss a ...
Kiss in softspots on ...
we were kids we placed ...
now we say yes how n...
There all growing seed sow...
of the proven Lotus Lifts line...
we Rature know ...
we always say when opportunity K...
Door we open with ...
This is our friends 13 a an ...
To guide your spirit as it Asce...
Lifts Lifts! scribed

Peace
&
Be well

rget

y you lied

Been strong

o I can no

storm

ways been our rock

will be for fret

stop

member what you were

mom   brosh your

clean your room Iron your

sweep the floor

Do your homework

ook both ways before you cross

AND always use the proper

I Tellsch you these

se I Love you

Be grow

lled

Q: From the looks of it, some may say you are a "Mama's Boy." What does this poem "MOM" speak to and why?

—◊—

A: "MOM", very simply and literally, was inspired by my mother, and everything that she went through to ensure that I was going to be a man in society who could take care of himself and his family; a man that would hold his head up high and be proud. I wrote this to let society know that there are women in our world who can raise men to be good men. It speaks to how strong women are. It's a poem about strength and perseverance, it's a poem about love. It's about teaching generations to support each other no matter what.

Q: What is the most significant lesson that your mother taught you? What did you learn from her life's example?

—◊—

A: I learned to stand up tall, take responsibility for my actions, make the best decision I can make and move forward.

you fiel

you forget

ou cry

...he you lied

...s Been strong

...no I can ho

...form

ys been

...ll be

p

...r what

no sir

ur room

the flo

your

before

...nys us

you

I Love you

ll Be, grow

s willed one day

...un family.

MOM

Mom, why do you fret?
Son, why do you forget?

Mom, why do you cry?
Son, remember when you lied.

Mom, you've always been strong.
Son, I am weathered, I can no longer bear the storm.

Mom, you have always been our rock.
Son, I still will be, for that will never stop.
Always remember what you were taught.
Say yes ma'am
No sir
Brush your teeth
Clean your room
Iron your clothes
Sweep the floor
Do your homework
Look both ways before you cross.

Oh, and always use the proper fork.
I teach you these things because I love you.
A good man you will be
Grown
      Intelligent
           Strong willed
And one day with your own family.

Mom, why is it you're never home?
Son , I work three jobs,
Take care of you and your brother.
Cook dinner
Make breakfast
Iron clothes
Mop floors
Walk dogs
And I do it all alone.

All I ask is that you go to school
Get your education
That will be my motivation.
Enough for me to strive and push harder
Against this perpetual rock of resistance

Persistence is key

Fighting for what you want and need

Advances us to longevity.

Life is family

Family is life

As you grow older you will need me less

When you take for you hopefully the right woma

wife.

Mom, I will never stop needing you as I grow olde

to this crazy commercialization of our people

Basketball

Football

Baseball

Upn

Espn

When

     When

        When does it stop.

       Tik - Tok

          Tik-Tok

I have dad now to talk to.

Stop think relax and pray.

Mom, why do you cry?
Why do you say you're tired?
Don't give up now, its birthing time again.
Let's give life to new ideas with old values
Buy new houses
Drive new cars
Eat good food
Live like stars.
I will take care of you
On that you can depend.

Son, I have never been worried about you until now.
Be mindful
Stay prayerful
Be kind
Don't worship money
Keep your mind.
Go forward
Move ahead
I am tired.
Don't worry,
I will never be far behind.

Phone wh

Home

Son I w

Of you

cook Dinner

clothes wa

And I do

all i ask is the

get your Education

motivation enough

And Posh Hardon

Perpetual Rocce

persistence

Wet you want &

us to benefit. Life

family is Life. As

you will need he

He right woman as

Mom you I will

As i grow older

crazy comes

Best by

Beauty

with a brush or sponge
... in your
... pool of Beauty
... your Brilliance
And admire you from

... away, Tell Stories
and when, as Jamaican
besos para ti, mi amore

patterns change when
... clear I'm all about
albeit
every few years
... I keep inside from
Able to Hold you
Too. But what can I do
... ly Day Dream of us
to go Deeper inside
... presente, To me
with you, is more,) more or less

... I swear I'll keep
... is where you
Be!

I wake up

Q: MAKEUP sounds like a poem about true beauty. What is the message that you want to convey here?

—⁂—

A: To me, true beauty is the beauty that comes from within. It's God-given. People who think beautiful thoughts, will allow beauty to emanate from them. It is a part of their aura. What you think surrounds you; it becomes you. You are not what you eat; you are what you think because what you think, you consume. The poem is about Inner and outer beauty. When you analyze the concept of makeup—what are you "making up" for? What are you "apologizing" for? You're beautiful just as you are. Does your makeup enhance or does it hide your true beauty? Is it necessary or have we been taught that it is better than who we naturally are? This poem is about true inner and outer beauty. The beauty that comes from inside, and from the intention of a man and a woman's heart, and the physical beauty that comes from the inside of who we are. That's what it's about. There is no apology needed for being who you are.

PErfect

your Beauty

a brush or spunge

POOL OF Beauty

BRilliant

...e you

..., Tell

as ...

...Are ti...

change...

I'm all ...

...year's

inside fro...

OLD you

what can i

...eam of us

...r inside

...To me

...n or less

I'll keep

you

MAKE-UP

Make up for what?
You're perfect

You can never cover up your beauty.
Bind your essence with a brush or spunge.
I want to lunge in your pool of beauty.
Get wet within your brilliance.
Take a glance and admire you from a distance.

Let's dance the night away.
Tell stories about what, why and when.

As Jamaicans say,
Come again, besos para ti, mi amor,
It's you I adore.

My heart's rhythmic patterns change
When you're near,
It's clear
I'm all about you.

Society changes a little bit every few years

Reminds me of the tear
I keep inside
From the sorrow of not being able to hold you.
The seconds, minutes, and hours get old too.
But what can I do?

As time passes
I can only daydream of us
Living it up
Seeking to go deeper inside each others essence

It's your presence to me
I want to just be with you.
Let's lift it up.
Less is more
More or less
Thoughts of you beat in my chest.

I swear
I'll keep it there
No.

I'll keep it here with me.
That's where you'll be.
When I wake up from dreaming about
Your makeup.

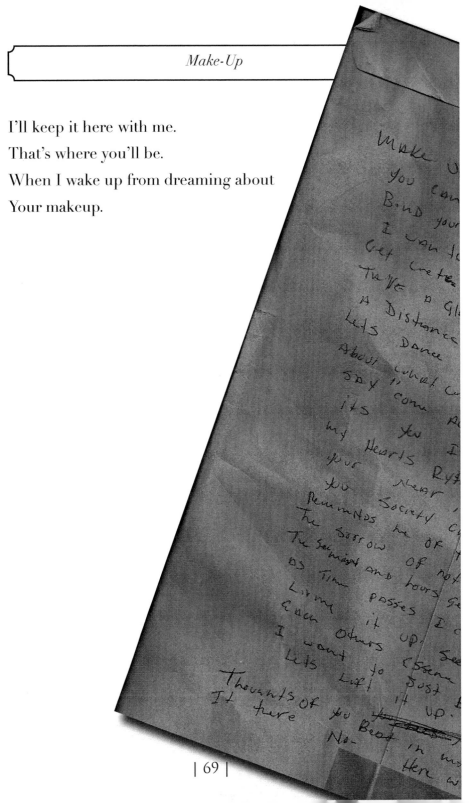

...nce

...e Because it makes

Happy I Dance Because

...ts me free Because

...I Dance I Dance

...d of Dance

...e the sun it

...or inspires strength

...ies, its

...I take it

...one a Day.

...play I have

...my romance

...I Love me

...it.

...in her

...cts me

...rta

Rythm

Q: The title of this next piece is called I DANCE. You are known around the world as an incredible choreographer. Tell us what your most provocative moment was in life as it relates to dance?

—⏀—

A: In 1995, I was chosen to work with Michael Jackson who was my lifelong inspiration. From childhood to young adulthood. In 1995, I was blessed to go to Hungary and work with him directly, and that was a pivotal moment in my career. It literally was a dream-come-true. Dance was the catalyst that brought me to that angel. And it was an indescribable year of my life. I was able to work directly with the King of Pop. We shared the love of dance together and it was an indescribable time. Dance is and was that spiritual transfer to physical embodiment that protected me, housed me, moved me and inspired me to express myself the way that I did.

I play row...
Lasting row...
. It love me
. Love it.
...lds hm in her
...und protects me
...ims me Birta
...un ...in, Rytum
...ge s...
a
...
...l R...
Devils
...

I DANCE

I dance because it makes me happy

I dance because it sets me free

I dance

       I dance

              I dance.

The spirit of dance is like the sun it gives life

Inspires strength

       Glows

              Fortifies

                     It's my vitamin

I take it more than once a day.

I dance

       I play

              I have a long lasting romance with it.

I love me and I love it.

She holds me in her womb

And protects me

Then she gives me birth

Again and again.

She raises me with rhythm.

It is a never ending vibration that transcends.

Culture

Race

Male and female

Genders

Boundaries

Height

Weight

And even missing limbs.

This is for her and him

They and them

I dance because I'm happy.

I dance because it frees me

I dance because it's inside me.

Pouring out like a stream of musical notes.

Rising to cocaphony of sounds and energy.

Popping

Locking

Hip hop

Modern jazz

Tap

Ballet

Interpretive

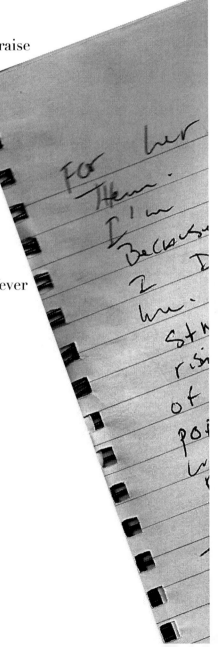

I Dance

Breaking the floor with the vibration
That comes from our feet
The unique ones
Always make the hair on your arm raise
Don't be alarmed
We're just dancing.
Crumping
Being free
Let's see you release
Try it.

Just for a moment in time.
It wont take any time to catch the fever
You'll never leave her.
She'll never leave you.
Do what you do.
  Dance
    Dance
      Dance

AS MUCH/AS you

much AS you can

a B power try tell

ed of lies / I know knowlese-

y potential power

a light in the tower Dim

ith electricity or no Battery

er must use what we them

et what WE wanT

must learn ourselves into

cess, powerT Happiness, where To

rn How to when to what To!

learn when not to.

who not to.

were not to. Learn.

Learn.

Learn.

Help Help your selves

of knowleda-

to S

Q: You have learned so much by looking at life through a child's eyes. So these next two poems are about children. Share with me how these poems have taught you about life.

—∞—

A: Children are my heart. They are innocent, sweet, and they are the future. They have taught me to be patient with myself, they have taught me to accept things in life in order to become stronger, to be quiet and to watch, and to listen before I speak. They have taught me to laugh again, they have taught me how to be proud of progress and process, and they remind me every day, to look for the child in me.

LEARN AS MUCH AS YOU CAN

Learn as much as you can.

Knowledge is power they tell me

I'm tired of lies.

I know knowledge is only potential power.

Like a light in the tower.

Dim from little electricity or no battery power.

We must use what we have to get what we want.

We must learn ourselves into success.

Power happiness, learn how to, when to.

Where to, what to.

Learn when not to, who not to.

Where not to.

     Learn

        Learn

          Learn.

Self help? Help yourselves!

To a cup of knowledge.

Use your actions

To stir a cup of mental powered coffee.

They lied and said

What you know will hurt you

I tell you what you don't know will hurt you.

Your money, they say

Hide your money in a book

I say keep 'em broke.

     Keep em broke

          and shook.

Read

     Read

          Read.

Til you get mental cramps and bleed.

Bleed new life into yourselves.

Bleed strength

Intelligence

Knowledge

Actions

Motivation

Determination.

Learn to dream and believe.

Learn to achieve

And receive the blessings.

From learning and taking action.

They lied and said
what you know will hurt
you, I tell you
what you don't know wil
they kill you.
I say keep em in a book
they said hide it in a book
Read
Read
Til you get mental cramps
Read
feed new Bleed into
your selves, bleed into
telligence + Bleed strength
vation + knowledge action
anticipation
rn to Dream of
lieve learn to Bless
cau to Bless
learn

HARD WORKERS

ok BOOKS AND MORE BOOKS

lne called Home

s wrappers from OlD

SODa. Bottle of unmentioned

~sht Coca cola.

ibriated child of the most

s not leaving the Books on

Down

AD

cac

ts 8

uese

a B

Yo

le

Bec

Birdy

Wom to a few min a

Ding is post Reed

y Brother Kms Andi

http://mail

FUTURE KINGS AND QUEENS

Children of the future
Royalty flowing from our bloodlines
Majestic thoughts that permeate the air.
Seated on thrones of responsibility
Leading the masses with empathy,
Love and accountability.

Is it you that I should look up to?
Are you ready for the challenge of this seat?
Pens and pencils scribed on papers
Checked once
       Checked twice
To make sure they're perpetually neat
Right for the reading.

This is a socially exalted place
Where the hard workers roam all day
Classes, books and more books
Studying in the place we call home:

Our dorm room.

Piles of clothes, wrappers from old sugar rush highs

Cans of soda

Bottles of unmentioned...or well should I say?

I wasn't Coca-Cola.

Definitely educated, sometimes inebriated

Child of the Most High

Seeking to better ourselves

Not leaving the books on the shelves

But taking them down and reading them.

Reading them, til' we get mental cramps and bleed

Because we plan on fulfilling the sociological need

Of a new day,

A new way.

I know it starts with me, with us, with we.

I choose to be the king, that queen

That creates a better world for the masses

The following question you may or may not ask is:

How can I serve you?

How can I use this seat?

I am a king, I am a queen, because I choose to be

Constitution using law-abiding liberty

It's about you, us, it's about we.

Forgive me, sometimes I'll have to take a few minutes out for

Facebook

Those are my needs.

Reading a post, read by most,

Just writing a few things

About my brothers and my sisters,

The Future Kings and Queens.

Throne

...my own Thrown That means I am
...be the president of the united Stat...
...sun west Wing, sitting up High
...Resett my Dome about the work
...to thrown into the universe
...lowthin the next verse
I DO I Do it for Pan-
...energetice moment moments
...the Stress for somm I take
...it my actions Traction bunds
...astion Days before weather
...one's that- or my feet mov...
...floor I knew you want
...Aknowledging my gifts
...HeaD to my toes
...dome Sounds of Brilliant
...erword Hear Back
...remove the Negative
...phorical necks
...ent fills my mind
...y Brothers an...

155548&view=att&th=1371401d2ad64af0c&attid_0.1&disp=inline&zw

Q: The poem, THRONE, could mean many things. How do you see yourself in light of this piece? How do you respond to people who call you cocky or arrogant?

—⁓—

A: *A car is a great thing because it can get you to and from places; it can get you there in a short or fast amount of time. But you can also take a car, start it and it can move without a person behind it. It can be very destructive. I think we have to be sure of ourselves, but also balanced and humble. Muhammad Ali was very sure about what he would be able to do in the ring. There are things that I know that I am sure about. When it came to dancing, I choreographed dance routines, concerts and award shows as if I was at war. Many people didn't know that but for me, it was war. I refused to lose. I take a page from LL Cool J, he said, "Mama said knock you out," and that's how I approached my life. I knew I was going to be the best on that stage. That's how I approach everything. Johnny Cochran once said, "let no one out-prepare you." Never let anyone out-prepare you. So, if that is cocky to be prepared and to know you're prepared because you know there is always another test, then the only people who would be against me that are the ones who want to put me in duress because they are not prepared.*

e

n That th...

sident of

st ving

my

throun

This the

DO I

energetic

em the

ry for m

wonewort

m Samo...

ally on the...
Here goes Aknowled...
in top of my Head to my ro...
ring in my Dome sounds of 16...
Moving forward Never Back
...uses remove the Negative
...lophorical necks
...T fills my win...
AND SISTE...

Silk=RG4790554&view=att&th=13...

THRONE

If I have my own throne
That means I'm a King
I might not be the President of the United States
But I have my own west wing.
Sitting up high,
Revelations reach my dome
About the work that needs to be thrown into the universe.
I will explain in this next verse:

I love what I do, I do it for fun
Get paid for energetic movements
Moments that relieve stress for some
I take responsibility for my actions
Traction builds from my movements
From days before
Whether I'm speaking someone's truth
Or my feet moving rhythmically on the floor
I know you want more so here it goes:

Acknowledging my gifts
From the top of my head to the bottom of my toes
Ideas ring in my dome
Sounds of brilliant A-tones

Moving forward, never back
Overlooking the masses
Removing the negative noose
Around our metaphorical necks

What's next?
Wonderment fills my mind
Thinking about, you, my brothers and sisters,
In this never ending universe
Expansive
Thought provoking
Stopped in your tracks
Went down the wrong pipe
Choking.

Think about seeds you have sown
As I observe up high
Receiving,

Learning,

    Yearning,

        For more time

            ...on my throne.

ACKNOWLEDGE SELF

is part child, part
adult part who
are Now acknowledge all
you are I, we are you
us. Dont fear! Run
towards the needless run
towards the beautiful energy
within for you run to share
yourself Nothing Being taken
only shared mmmmmmmm
reciprocation Be filled Never
empty always abundantly
filled Be open to the
Now you have been led
here to express the real you
not the you we thought
knew Like a yes length
Re-new Like a yes length of car
registration Drive the
truck motorcycle or
to speed talk
others

Q: ACKNOWLEDGE SELF is about so many things. Tell me in a few words what the core pieces are to this poetic puzzle.

—⁂—

A: *This poem is about acknowledging God, acknowledging his creation, which is me. Acknowledging cause and effect. Acknowledging choice. Acknowledging my heartbeat. Acknowledging my breathing pattern. Acknowledging my seven layers of skin. Acknowledging my bloodline; the height that I have; the width of my chest; the brownness of my skin; acknowledging the endless and ever-expanding universe that I am apart of. It's about acknowledging self.*

ACKNOWLEDGE SELF

We are part child
Part young adult
Part who we are now
Acknowledge all of you.

The I
    The you
        The we
           The us.

Don't fear
Run towards the newness
Run
Catch the beautiful energy waiti
Run to share yourself.

Nothing being taken
Only shared mmmm.
Reciprocation
Be filled

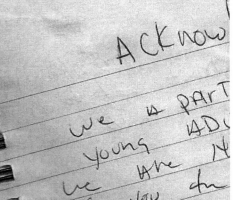

Never empty.

Always abundantly filled.
Be open to the now.
You have been led here
To express the real you
Not the you we thought we knew.

Renew like a year's length.
Registration
Drive the car
The pick-up truck
The motorcycle of life

No need to speed.
Take heed
Learn from others.
Mistakes
Remember when to pump the brakes.

All that you need
You already have
Smile

Don't get mad

Acknowledge the God in you.

soul of wh

soul of a mon
where it Does it LIVE
is it in his stride
r in the crook in his
ye. The way He walks
the Vibrato as he talks
it his strong arms
his strength in his
s. Is is the momentary
ts of courage that
often or for in
is it His
AND in His Lean?
the way He
His
almient bless.
your

Q: THE SOUL OF A MAN. This is a more introspective poem. Everyone wants to know what the true soul of a man or a woman really is. Talk to us about it from your perspective.

—⁂—

A: In my opinion, the true soul of a man or a wo-man is the essence of that individual; it's the spirit; it's the style, vibration of their voice; a shape of a woman; her kindness; her ability to raise a child and sit and rub that child's head when it's sick. It's the determination that a man wakes up with in the morning to take care of his family. It's his thoughts; it's the energy of the sun that energizes him; it's his/her way of communicating; it's being able to understand what one sees through someone else's eyes. It's their essence… the energy that we know to be them.

Of Woman

Does it LIVE

His Stride

come in

His

eng

is

Cou

r

#

He's Lean?

by He

t blessed

Head

THE SOUL OF A MAN

Where does it live?

Is it in his stride

Or in the wink of his eye?

The way he walks

Or the vibrato as he talks?

Is it his strong arms?

Or the strength of his palms?

Is it the momentary choice of courage that comes often or far

in between?

Maybe it's his smile & his lean

Is it the way he cooks or His God given,

Almighty Blessed,

You can rest your head on his chest good looks?

Is it his silence when he thinks?

Or is it his generosity?

Before you answer STOP and THINK

Maybe it's inside...

Inside the 7 layers of skin behind flesh and blood

Dwelling in the place we call home

(Our inner self)

That sweet
    Deep
        Silent place
Where there is no color or race
This is where it is
Yea
Knowing what I am and must be..
A boy til I grow old.

This I stand
A man
In agreement with my soul

generosity

up you answer

& Think.

its inside

re 7 layers of skins

flesh & bone

in fact

call Home.

her Self Place

Deep sile

there is

...ep DARK chocolate
...K chocolate Like Fre
... coms from the Ground
...olate soft What a lonely
... Hous I gonna Damn you
... in the cnd We all see
...und so why not
...is amazing Beautiful
... Phentatyful more than enough
... in the mouth of Honds
... sugary taste of 960s
... chocolate, Brown even Brown
...sted Brown US Board of cDucation,
... mom a lonely sand'tmokes when We Imagine
...Brown on top of Brown you ask
... Hous it goin Down know...
... I trount you will I'll fill you in about the
... Brown mom from the Boogm DA
... this is Hou it went Down
... Born in earth DAY
... as my mothers Birth
... on Life.

Q: DEEP DARK CHOCOLATE- since we are already "deep" in our moments of introspection, explain what Deep Dark Chocolate is about? What does it acknowledge? And Why?

—⁓—

A: *Deep dark chocolate is about loving the skin that I'm in. It's about looking and seeing me in others. It's about seeing me in the future. It's about acknowledging a Continent that I've never been to physically. It's about desires and dreams. It's about fighting through adversity. It's about smiling and holding a child with your hand stretched in the air and praising the Almighty for a newborn. It's about acknowledging the dirt that we come from and the dirt that we shall return to.*

DEEP DARK CHOCOLATE

Like the color that comes from the ground
Milk chocolate
Soft
What a lovely color brown.
How's it going down, you ask?
Well in the end, we all see the ground.
So why not love this amazing, beautiful ,strong ,plentiful
,more than enough, Melts in your mouth and in your hands
Sweet sugary taste of God's created chocolate.
Brown man, Brown woman,
Brown vs. Board of Education.
What a lovely sound it makes when I imagine
Brown on top of brown.

How's it going down you ask?
Well, I thought you knew
Well I'll fill you in about the brown man
from the boogie down,
This is how it went down.

I was born

my Earth day was the same day as my mother's birthday

GET IT? MY DELIVERY TO EARTH -DAY MOTHER GAVE BIRTH-DAY!

we both agreed on life.

My mother carried, labored, pushed hard

SHE Delivered without the knife. No incisions were made. It was a beautiful birth.

Named by my grandma, Darrin Dewitt Henson, welcome to earth.

The Bronx is where I call home. The Home of Hip Hop ,where the culture really roams Cardboard boxes, JVC bi-phonics.

Back in the day we called them Radios, who the fuck named them Boom Boxes?

Chuck taylors on my feet.

Harlem was crowded with fiends, usually from what I can remember on 116 Street,

Afrika Bambaataa Planet rock was playing,

B-boys in the park.

Poppers are poppin. Rhymers sayin, "yes yes y'all, to the beat
y'all."
You know what I'm talking about. You've heard it before.
It's historical info so listen… Here goes some more
Dip dip dive so-socialize, clean out your ears and open your
eyes
In this social environment, government tells us lies
to disguise the beast inside
 But we see you
and we know who you are
When I was a child, I wished upon stars.
But now it's all about hard work and dedication.
Human beings sucked by the prostitute of inflation
Wear your condoms
protect your minds
because this society wants what's yours and mine.

By the place I call home
Sheridan, Noble Ave. Parkchester, Blackrock Ave.
These places I did roam
Rested my head, prayed, ate meals and changed clothes.
Created body of work the whole world knows.
Chorography in my living room day and night

Getting the job done.

Man! it felt so right!

From the Bronx to Hollywood it's all inside me

There is stuff trapped in spite of me!

Doing what I needed to do to release but I can't let go

my best friend passed away in 9-11.

His name was Steve Mercado.

I love you always and still you're around.

Always knew you'd be heaven bound

Protector of many

 father of two.

Best friend to me

 I will always love you!

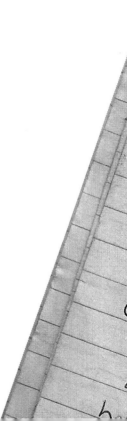

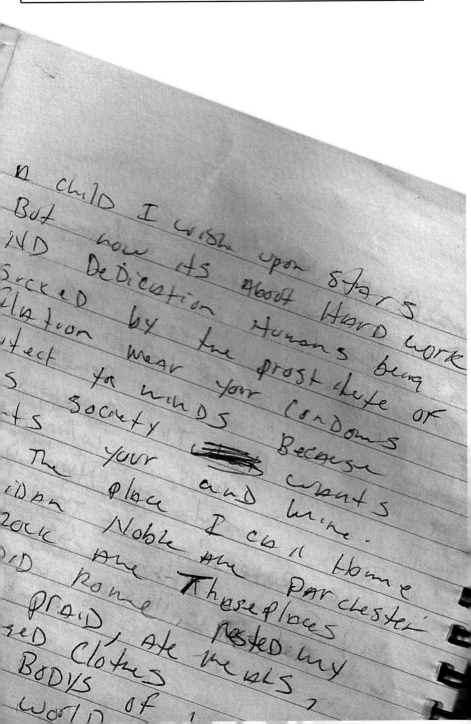

a child I wish upon stars
But now its about Hard work
AND Dedication Humans being
sucked by the prostitute or
elation wear your condoms
itect to minds Because
its society ~~that~~ wants
The your and mine.
iopa place I call Home
zock Noble are Parchester
oD Rome Theseplaces
praid Ate me als?
sed clothes Rested my
BODYS of
world

t will a man Gain
He Loses his SOUL!
food that we Harvist
our brains Does it
or Does it rot or
us a GOOD thing
it most Definately
Life? we Should
away from the Decey
the Negptive, Rise
bone...meet & Greet that
lluminus light of
ositive. This is where
can ~~~~ Live.
OOD for thought is what
was taught, Eat some
that GOOD GOOD!
Remove the HOOD
or places

Q: WHAT WILL A MAN GAIN IF HE LOSES HIS SOUL? Clearly you can answer this question with the exposure and success you have experienced. Talk to me about your experience with success and the consequences of it.

—◦◦◦—

A: I've seen people end up in jail for the rest of their lives for making the wrong choice. There have been people who have been sentenced to prison for speaking up with their strong voice; people who have compromised integrity only to gain financial wealth. This poem is about me watching our society implode from greed –it's about not saying yes to failure. It's about saying YES to success; saying yes to HELP. It's about knowing that we can overcome any adversity.

...t will a man gain
If he Loses his sou...
The food that we He...
our brains
...it... ...is or Does...
...Li...
...way...
Ne...
...light...
...is 13
Ne...
...t is what
...t some

...ces
...Han...

WHAT WILL A MAN GAIN IF HE LOSES HIS SOUL?

The food that we harvest for our brains

Does it remain as a good thing?

Will it most definitely bring life?

We should move away from the decay of the negative,

Rise above

Meet and greet that illuminouss light of positivity.

This is where we all can live.

Food for thought is what I thought

Eat some of that Good Good

Remove the hood

Whether the suburbs

Or place you only go if you have the nerves

Want that good fight

It's our plight, our struggle

Remove the rubble that has been placed before you

To make you trip and slip

Take a sip of that Good Good

We'd get sugared iced teas in the hood

Beeds of sweat

Fall down our necks

Jumped rope

    Feens lost hope

What will a man gain if he loses his soul?

Doesn't it get old?

Watching youth grow not knowing about tomorrow

Energy that forever flows

Who knows?

    Is it an odyssey?

        As we watch commodities

It never gets old

But what will a man gain if he loses his soul?

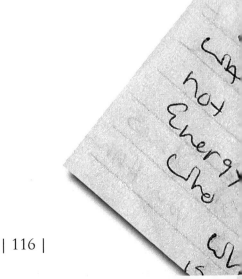

I aint that goo
Its our phight ou
remom the rubble th
Has been placed before
you to wake you trip & sli
Twice. a sip of that good
Good. We-D get suppres
I ced teas in the hood
Beeps of sweat jumped rope
our Necks jouped rope what
s shot Dope gwin If He
t His soul.
it get old?
you the

HEAD ACHES FROM
the negative vibratory
Quakes.

monson is coming soon
seal the Negative Doom
it Lift up catch the
of the rising god
Above the Negative smog
through the heavywinds

sitive force create your
D winds, learn
as you can to change
Like a Dance
Dance
little to change
with me
lls are free
from the Bone
search for

Q: LIFT- where were you when you wrote that poem? What were you thinking about?

—⟁—

A: I was on a US air flight flying from the east coast to the west coast. I remember watching CNN in between terminals. There were talks of war on every station. And I just remember wanting them to turn off the TV sets. Everywhere you went, CNN was talking about war and it saddened me. It upset me because we were being forced to listen to something that we didn't want to listen to. I felt forced because, unless you had headphones on, you couldn't tune it out. I really wanted to tune out the negativity. There are so many good things to report that we never hear. It doesn't seem to find its way onto the media. So this poem was a mental aspirin for me. I was writing to stop my head from aching. That is why I wrote the poem "Lift."

LIFT

My head aches
From the negative vibratory quakes
A monsoon is coming soon
To seal the negative doom.

I say lift up
catch the spirit of the rising god
Lift above the negative smog.
Smile through the heavy winds
Be a positive force.
Create your own head winds.
Leave as little as you can to chance.
Move through life like a dance.
Dance
      Dance
          Dance.
Leave very little to chance.

Sit back fly with me
Where the angels are free.

Free yourselves from the bondage of doubt.

Search for truth.

That's what it's all about.

Your skin tingles from the possibilities of joy

Your mind wonders as a child who

Plays with its favorite toy.

Fly I say

      Fly

            Ever so high

See over them.

Rise and live in the sky.

Believe.

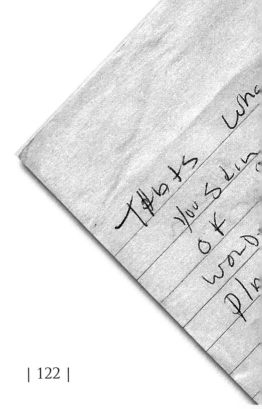

All About!

from possibilities

your mind who

as a child who

its favorite toy.

Fly I say Fly.

so high SEE over

Rise and live in

sky. Believe!

AWARD

I Never walked on the moon
But I have a moon man.
Dancing and Choreography
W placed this with moon
my Hand
with silver gu) Holding a
would spark a flame
ME that I always had
fire grew inside.
ngt & stronger so much
I could no Longer
this Flame
would Educate me
This world called fame
e "way you make me feel
it to you Bye By Bye
ce the whole

Q: Your poems "DREAMS" and "AWARD" go hand in hand. One depicts a picture of your standing in front of the HOLLYWOOD sign. Another depicts you standing there to receive your MTV Award. Explain to me how your dreams and awards have reshaped your life.

—⚹—

A: I used to imagine myself being able to stand in the middle of the street and see the HOLLYWOOD sign, but as a kid growing up in NY, I used to think that Hollywood was as far away as the moon is. But in actuality, all you have to do is get on a plane and get in the middle of the street. If you can get there mentally, you can get there physically. Anything in life is attainable and achievable. I wanted to get to Hollywood and here I am. And the MTV award that I received was for choreographing Nsync's "Bye Bye Bye." But for me, I received the award in remembrance of and appreciation for all the other work that came before that award. Without those works, I wouldn't have been prepared to receive that award. Both of these poems were written in acknowledgment of the dreams I had before I was able to see them manifest.

Bright
will
the stars
the earth
below
or show
remmours
to our
Dream
our
it
HOLLYWOO

DREAMS

"Dreams Do Come True"

…Just have faith…

Remember that word?

Most people seem to forget what they were taught as a child.

"But the children shall inherit the earth."

Give birth to the past teachings.

Once again, let it ring in your ear like a bell

But don't be late for class

Let your mind expand with the speed of light

Make way for the new old you

Renew your promise of excellence of passion

Of using your gift

I nothing more than

To uplift everything in your energy field

Peace

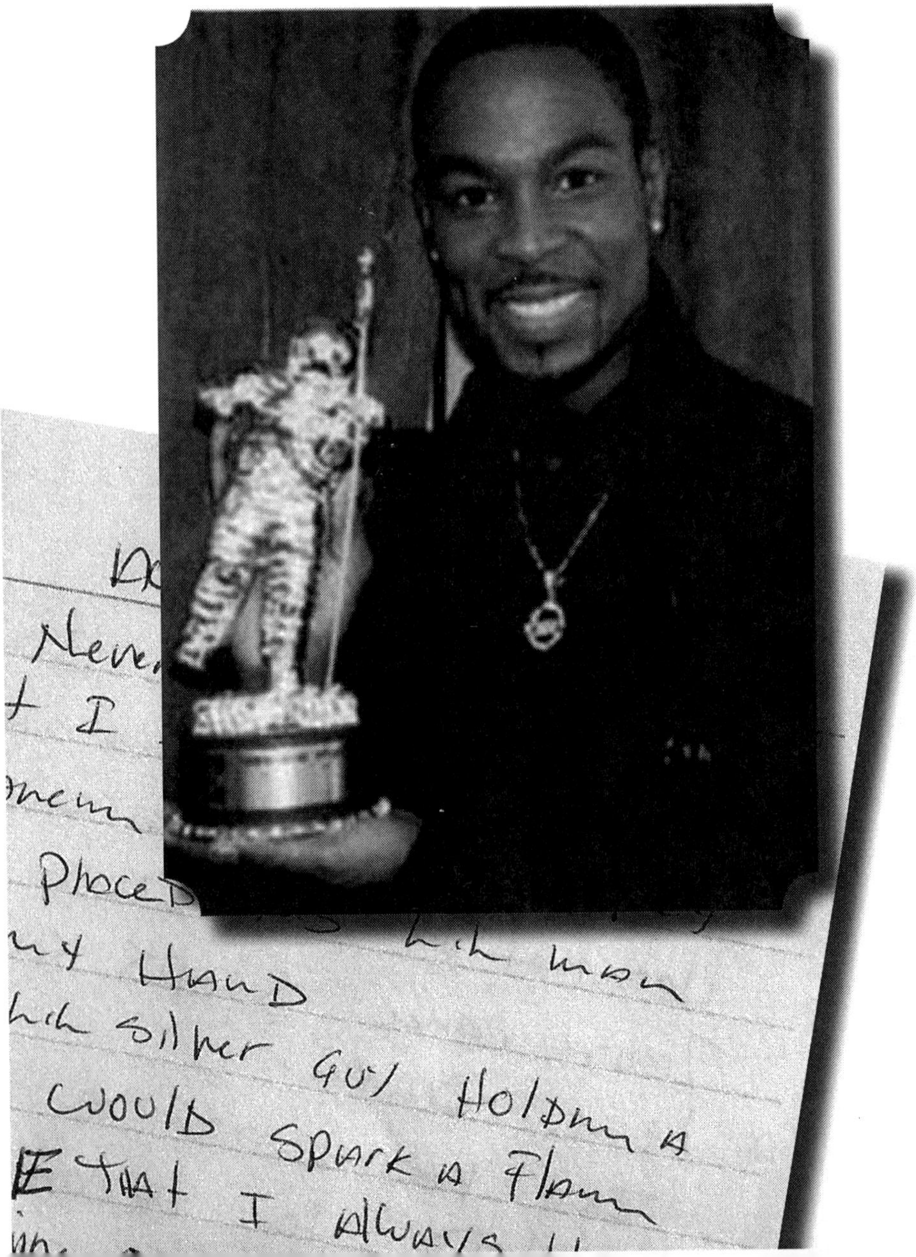

Never
HAND
silver guy
would spark a
that I always

AWARD

I never walked on the moon
But I have a moon man
Dancing and choreography
Now place this little man in my hand
This little silver guy holding a flag
Would spark a flame in me
I always knew I had

This fire grew inside
Stronger and stronger
So much
That I could no longer control this flame
It couldn't hide.

That would educate me
About this world called fame
Hmm.
From "The way you make me feel"
To "Give it to You."

To "Bye, Bye, Bye."

Is a dance the whole world would do

The MTV stage was created for me

A choreographer, I knew I would be

Watching Rhythm Nation,

I copied the dance without hesitation

Feeling alive,

those dance steps

Created a brand new drive

In me was a seed planted

To become one of the best

One enchanted with the gift

Souls I would lift

    And lift

        And lift

With the movements that came from inside

    I laughed

        I wondered

            I smiled

                I cried

All the emotions I had inside

Wanting the award

Knowing God gives the reward

I stay true to me
Wanting what I knew was due
That would be mine,
From MTV

My moon man
And that ain't no lie.
Bye
       Bye
            Bye.

As I Realize -

Love is what Happens as
I Realize - Who I really am
Opening a Door for a Lady
Or saying yes ma'am.
Doing something Just because
Its Right. Smiling stating
Thank you. or you as well
Wish you a Good night

I Realize. a Better Thru
accounts of robert animosity
tomorrow. There is Strength
Today is renewed here
can see a new you
down the Streets of Possibility
who came before what was
our use. without shame
loud Strong and misunderstood
me Been or Should
what i Can Do
We H

Q: AS I REALIZE is about epiphanies and spiritual observations. Talk to me about this heavenly and inspirational poem, and why it means so much to you.

—⅏—

A: *This came after a day of meditating with a shaman who taught me to pay attention to the trees. The trees do what their supposed to do—give oxygen, receive carbon and they are beautiful yet strong. When we relax in life, we are able to take in more. We are able to understand. We are able to make better decisions. We realize that nothing stays the same. Things are forever changing. It is a poem about consciousness. This is why it means so much to me. We are what we think. When we realize that, we open ourselves to new realities and new possibilities.*

Notairy for
built.
or guilt PROUD
what COULD Hove Bee
As I realize what i
As I reorize what
Doesn't matter we Ho
work from Dow
the BRIDG
Amy

AS I REALIZE

Love is what happens
As I realize who I really am.
Opening a door
For a lady or saying yes ma'am
Doing something just because it's right.
Smiling
Saying thank you
Or you as well

I wish you a good night.
As I realize a better tomorrow
No thoughts of regret
      Animosity
            Or sorrow.
There is strength in me today
A renewed me
So I can see a new you.
Walking down the streets of possibility.
Noticing who came before
What was built for our use

Without shame or guilt
Proud
    Strong
        And misunderstood.
What could have been or should?
As I realize what I can do.
As I realize what I must.
Doesn't matter, we have to put in work, from dawn til dusk?
Building the bridges in and out minds
Laying the foundation
That will stand the test of time.
I notice the trees all neatly growing
in a line
Still tall and beautiful as I realize.

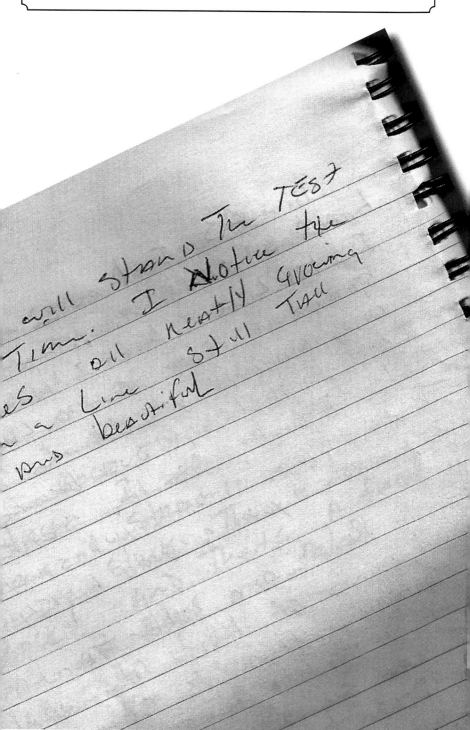

will stand The TEST
Time. I Notice the
es all Neatly growing
a Line still Tall
and beautiful

Q: You end your first volume of INTIMATE THOUGHTS with a poem titled FEAR. What is the underlying message you want to convey to others about FEAR?

—⁂—

A: Upon writing this book I realized how long it took me to do it. This is something I've been wanting to do for well over 20 years, but I let fear keep me from flying. I allowed fear to get in the way. And now I see fear differently. I know that fear is only a perilous disease that will keep you incarcerated in failure. The message is simple: "Don't fear, fear." If I can do it, why can't you? Fear isn't real.

FEAR

FEAR

F-alse

E-vidence

A-ppearing

R-eal

Don't fear fear.
It's not real.

ACKNOWLEDGMENTS

Thank You to my mom, dad, brothers - Maurice ,Frank Jr., Mark, Daryl, and Charles.

My three sisters, Byan, Mayattu and Ilam
My Children - Esai, Dhaamin, Nia, Triston, and Kiina
My Step Mothers Cookie and Asha
My Friend - Evelyn V.

Uncle Timmy and Uncle Sam, Aunt Fran, and Uncle Gary
Cousins Kim, Andrea and Artie
Adesola Osakalumi and Antoine Judkins

Felicia Henderson - *Thank you for believing in me!*

Sharon Jackson - *Thank You for having my back for so many years!*

Dr. Robert Johnson, Dr. Maurice A. Lee - *COUNTLESS THANK YOU'S*

Jim Brown - *To know you, listen and learn from you - PRICELESS!*

Hugo Huizar - *Couldn't have done it without you!*

Thanks to Michael Jai White and Imanni Lee for having my back in the Ring!

Shaun and Ana Saunders, *for helping me publish my intimate thoughts!*

LOVE TO ALL! DDH

FOR SPEAKING ENGAGEMENTS AND APPEARANCES

E-mail ddgmail1@aol.com

www.darrinhenson.com